The Ways We Touch

The
Ways
We
Touch

Poems by

Miller Williams

University of Illinois Press

Urbana & Chicago

Manufactured in the United States of America

Limited Edition printing, January 1997

This book is printed on acid-free paper.

Thanks to the editors of the following
publications in which some of these
poems have appeared:

The Kenyon Review: "If Ever There Was One";
    "Listen"; "On Word That the Old Children's
    Stories Have Been Brought Up to Date";
    "Wide Place in the Road"
Image: "God"
The Southern Review: "A Lesson on the
    Twentieth Century"
New Orleans Review: "As You Both Shall Live,"
    "Origami," "71 South"

Library of Congress
Cataloging-in-Publication Data

Williams, Miller.
The ways we touch : poems / by Miller Williams.
    p. cm.
ISBN 0-252-02362-5 (alk. paper)
I. Title.
PS3545.I53352W3   1997
811'.54—dc21
96-51233
CIP

. . . and for Jordan,
as always.

Contents

Part 3:   Admonitions

Part 4: The Inaugural Poem

Part 1

Rumors

By what cross purposes
the world is dreamt.
—Richard Wilbur

I heard the dust falling
between the walls.
—Howard Nemerov

Listen

I threw a snowball across the backyard.
My dog ran after it to bring it back.
It broke as it fell, scattering snow over snow.
She stood confused, seeing and smelling nothing.
She searched in widening circles until I called her.

She looked at me and said as clearly in silence
as if she had spoken,
I know it's here, I'll find it,
went back to the center and started the circles again.

I called her two more times before she came
slowly, stopping once to look back.

That was this morning. I'm sure that she's forgotten.
I've had some trouble putting it out of my mind.

A Lesson on the Twentieth Century

They rode around in auto-mobiles,
metal sitting rooms that sat on wheels
and coursed a network of concrete
laid down by labor, a grid of street across street
inside the cities, and on the countryside
long winding ribbons sometimes laid so wide
eight of the units could run along together,
half going one direction and half the other.
The engines that powered them were built to burn
the residue of ancient life. You'll learn
now if you will activate your screens
how the drivers of these ingenious machines
could shift the ratios of their mechanical gears.
A lot of things have altered over the years
since nations went to war for gods and lands
and things lived in the oceans and there were bands
of people who used their own breath and hands
to make their music. All this was long before
we freed ourselves from fretting about chance
and learned not to walk too close to the shore
or think about things like dolphins anymore.

4

It Came to Pass on a Planet Third
from a Minor Sun in a Solar System
Out on the Edge of One of the Galaxies

If there are intelligent beings
in some other place
did Jesus go to be born
and die for them there?
If he didn't
are they still offered the grace
of God and if they aren't
is that fair?

Autopsy

Here in a place where much
was hated and held dear
you feel no part of yes
no matter what you touch.

There isn't a soul here,
only an empty house in a brambly lot.
But is there not a forwarding address?
No, there is not.

Woman with Dog

Walking along a beach on St. George Island
where two men fished for sea trout under the surf
he saw the track of a dog with paws so big
it must have weighed a hundred pounds or more,
a trail so narrow no print was out of line
by half its width. You don't often see, he said,
a dog like that, of such great weight and grace.

There joined and left and crossed the track of the dog
the deep meandering prints of someone running,
more loping than jogging—the feet fell farther apart,
the heels sunk into the sand a little more deeply.
The shoes were new, by their treads, and smaller than his.

With legs too long for a child, this was a woman,
a woman running, but less intent than her dog
on getting where they were going. And where was that?
And who waited there, to tell her what?
How glad would she be to be home, getting into the shower?

The prints were new, the newest on the beach.
No wave or wind or seabird track had touched them.
He tightened his eyes, wanting to see them running
and thought he did, maybe, against a dune
as far as he could focus. He saw something,
a group of gulls rising, and then nothing.

He looked for the trail to end at tire tracks
where blacktop curved into the beach, but it kept on going,
into the evening, farther than he could go
if he was going to be where he said he'd be
for dinner and talk and a fireplace and people he knew.
Already, when he turned back, the two men fishing
seemed so small in the distance they could have been driftwood.
Somewhere behind him the woman, not thinking of him.
Near the closed door, asleep, the magnificent dog.

A Thought as It Turns

Truly we have not been here long—twelve hours,
if you consider the age of the earth a year;
by the age of the universe, the beat of a heart.
That's likely half the time we'll have here
before we tuck it in and call it a day.

We sometimes feel uneasy, looking forward,
but won't feel too bad, maybe, looking back
to where, if we never outgrew our temper and fear
and visions left us blind and voices deaf,
still there was art a while, and math, and music,
forbearance and hope and wit and architecture,
and once this porch, and once this day, and you
at needlepoint slowly, guiding the needle through.

10,000-Year-Old Tree Discovered
Shades Two and a Half Acres

This tree took root before Jerusalem,
before Troy, before Constantinople,
before there were cities to name,
before there were farms,
the most ancient living thing on earth
for all we know,
which may mean also in the universe.
So listen to this and tell me
how it grabs you:

Come let us open the door
to your new home
where you can lead your guests across a floor
older than Rome.

I think Jerusalem is older but it doesn't rhyme.
Anyway, poets use Rome to mean a really long time.

He Shuts His Eyes
for the Layman's Long Prayer about Lust
and the Mind of the Young Preacher
Wanders Again

Say a man tells a woman that he was blind
from birth and lately found a medical chance
to see and took it,
say this is a lie he tells, a little pretense.

He means he therefore has the eyes of a child,
not having seen a woman naked. He knows
what she will do.
She is going to take off all her clothes.

Will he be blind in hell? Surely he will,
though will it matter when he's all afire?
Say there's a child.
The child did neither pleasure nor conspire

but guilt follows the flesh. His ancient book
will fall out of balance if God forgets.
No matter to Him
how hard we pray, God please, He collects His debts.

Pure love has little use for sentiment
and hope, if you live forever, must seem odd,
though maybe He tries
to love the ways we love. Please God.

At the Christening of an Infant
the Mind of the Young Preacher
Wanders Again

It's not for us to give this soul to God.
We're here to recognize that the soul is God's.
Rather, I want to say, the soul is God.
This is as doubtless and clear as the baby's eyes.

What swirls about me when I hold a thing
so recently a fish, a tadpole,
is a murky and restless thought: when came the soul?
It had to be at a moment. It couldn't have been
little by little. The mind is repelled, rebels
at the thought of sort of a soul, God tiptoeing in.

A sperm and an egg, each with half a soul,
is something equally noxious, when you consider
the countless that go for nothing.

                            Say the zygote,
the fertilized egg, gets a soul for the fact of that—
what if it doesn't grab hold and falls in the toilet?
Does that soul get another chance? If not,
where does it go? What does it know about being?

At viability, then? Is that the word?
And what exactly is that? Eleven-thirteen
on the second day of the twenty-fourth week?
I don't know if God can tell time.

I know there is a soul in this mass of cells.
I think I know when it leaves. May that be a long
and richly textured time from all of this.

Take our love and your chances. Take all your names,
your new one, and God, and human—and go forth.

The Affair

He lived in a double-wide and drove a truck,
drank a Pepsi-Cola at every meal,
read the obituaries and comic strips,
meant the center of everything he said,
listened to country music, laughed at jokes,
and bet a little on the football spread.

She lived in a high-rise and practiced law,
had coffee at breakfast, always three and black,
read the obituaries and business news,
meant both sides of everything she said,
listened to new jazz, smiled at wit,
and bet on the futures market, the price spread.

They spoke the same language, more or less,
but not to each other, of course, except for the time
when they were stuck alone in an elevator
for fifty minutes five years ago.
Though each was afraid of needing a bathroom
they both behaved the way they felt befit
the sudden circumstance. They tried to relax.
She totally missed his jokes and he her wit.

Now, though, making love to the dwindling few,
he thinks of her, the small hands and the scent.
In bed she imagines him, the mouth and the smell,
what he would want her to do, what he would do.

The Light in the Eyes

Who knows
where it goes?

Part 2

Errands

Love's austere and
lonely offices.
—Robert Hayden

Someone will have to stay
and sell the cows.
—Jo McDougall

On Word That the Old Children's Stories Have Been Brought Up to Date

The farmer's wife missed the tails entirely.
Jack and the giant became the best of friends.
The boy cried *wolf* again and the people came
but didn't hurt the wolf, just sent it thence.

Young Ms. Hubbard's cupboard was full of bones.
Humpty Dumpty bounced like a rubber ball.
The woman who lived in a shoe was kind to her kids.
Ms. Muffet was not afraid of spiders at all.

So now does Icarus flutter down to the sea
and swim ashore? Does Cyclops keep his eye?
Doesn't Achilles worry about his heel?
Are there no consequences? Does no one die?

Is this what we say to the kids—You can be bad,
but, hey, it's OK, nobody's going to get mad?

Personals

Like a challenge? Male, 45
could pass for 60, at least twice divorced,
heavy smoker, sober now and then,
living in trailer home with no water,
looking for female with good job.

We may have no more need for half our doctors
and every talk show will fold flat
when we can understand why there are people
who will enclose a picture and answer that.

Romance

First, of course, you think of Robin Hood,
partial to poor folk, unimpressed by power;
then the cat burglar, black slacks and sweater,
always unarmed, making clever remarks.
Then someone steps suddenly out of an alley
to take your cash and the ring that meant so much,
or the car has disappeared from the carport,
or you get home and someone has emptied the house
you promised to pay for in thirty years.
You imagine you have them in court. They show you hells,
bad fathers and broken homes, their mothers' tears.
They can die now, you say, or die in their cells.

A Note to the English Poets of the Seventeenth Century

Who is it who knows for sure
that we can't do this,
write back as well as forth,
send words both ways?
Some people in our time
have come to suspect
that time is less straightforward
than we had thought.

I would like to believe
that if I believed enough . . .
but that's no good.
If this gets through to you,
if ever it could,
then three hundred years ago it did.
And I, a student of everything you knew,
would certainly know.
So this was a fantasy
to be let go.

Here is something more likely, but barely so:
that someone rummaging here from a later time
may come across enough of this to guess
I wrote you meaning to answer your long question,
saying, Yes,
some of us still read you now and then,
as dead white men.

Who could ever have wanted more than this,
to be remembered and read
with students writing papers on your poems
three hundred years after you were dead?
Who wouldn't settle for that?
you might say.

We think we would,
but when we consider it more,
something maybe a little nobler than greed
measures how very small
is the space of a thousand years
compared to our honest need
and wonders why a name should run out at all
as long as people remember how to read.

The problem with that is that readers to come,
waiting in all the futures,
will have so many wanting to be remembered,
with every century thousands of dead poets
rattling their doors,
there won't be room in all their heads together.

Someone in every century has to stand there
saying, No, I'm sorry, I'm sorry,
I'm sorry.
You've gone as far as you can go.

Oh, Jonson, Herrick, Cowley, Waller, Carew,
Lovelace, Crashaw, Marvell,
Herbert, Traherne,
Suckling, Donne, and Vaughan,
most of you will be gone
from whatever pass for books
in years to come
and some

reading the three or four that make it through
will shake their heads and say,
as even now we do
(having I think already turned back a few),
"They didn't have many poets, but they were great."

Of course they were.
You've lost the ones that were hopelessly only good,
saying things that nobody else could say
and lucky to be heard in their own day.

I have had you often on my mind,
you from the sixteen hundreds
who've come this far.

It doesn't matter if all of this never loops out
of the timeline it's apparently written in.

Though I have admired your wisdom
and your skill,
it isn't really you I'm writing about.

Her, Though

It didn't come all at once, it didn't come easy,
deciding to try to find the off button.

It wasn't the humiliation of stumbling along
a murky neuron path looking for names
of people he saw every day. It wasn't the pain,
though more and more he imagined pans of water
boiling behind his eyeballs, his liver grilled.

Her, though, having to handle it all by herself
that's what it was. He thought and thought about it,
all the attention and money to be paid,
then her watching him fade to a poor suggestion
of something in her past. He was more afraid
of luring her into that than surprising her now
when he and the bank account both had a balance.

He thought of little else but doing it.
He wasn't sure that these were dark thoughts.
If they were dark he had them anyway,
though now and then he smiled or nearly smiled
to think of what doing it used to mean
in maybe the backseat of a Chevrolet
with what-was-her-name with the sweet-smelling hair,
something he'd thought about and thought about
the long year when he was seventeen,
something that somehow never did work out.

A Good Son

He called home every once in a while
to tell his mother,
just so he could imagine how she would smile,
something or other

about a girlfriend
or work or a new movie he might have seen,
whatever was right.
He lied some, but mostly he stayed between

fantasy and fact.
He was a good son. He loved his mother a lot
and knew what she needed—
to live through him whether he lived or not.

The Sissy

He's never been pointed to first for anything
except by the bony finger of the teacher
who knows he'll have his homework done and perfect
which makes him so ashamed he'd like to fail
but knows that failing would leave him here even longer.

He tries to catch a ball and he wants to die.
Sometimes he lies in bed and thinks of dying,
forcing out some last important words
just before his head falls back on the pillow
or rolls out of the hand of whoever holds it
onto the carpet or grass or saddle blanket
leaving those people that never knew who he was
to look at one another in dusty silence.

A Christmas Poem

In a little bar on the Gulf Coast
someone offers a Christmas toast.
The piano player, believe it or not,
plays "As Time Goes By." Almost.

The bartender brings over a lot
of nuts and crackers. I have a shot
of Jack to get me on my way.
After a while, it's *What have you got?*

A drunk counts out some coins to pay
for a bottle of wine. He stops to say,
How are you doing? The syllables stink.
I lift my glass to say, I'm OK.

Out of the corner what I think
is a man in a wig and a ratty mink
weaves his way across the floor
and buys the piano player a drink.

At a table for two close to the door
a man seems to mean to ignore
a woman chewing a wad of gum.
The bartender brings me a couple more.

The piano player plays us some
of what the season wants. We hum
along and call for more and then
a man at the bar takes his thumb

out of his mouth and says there are ten
minutes left, Good will to men.
Good men, a woman says, to me.
He puts his thumb in his mouth again.

I manage a toast to the Christmas tree
and one to the sweet absurdity
in the miracle of the verb to be.
Lucky you, lucky me.

He thinks he wouldn't have thought for all those miles
about the squirrel but shrugged and said, Tough luck,
if it hadn't been for the acorn he saw in its mouth
when it turned confused to face the truck.

I'm sorry, I'm really just too tired tonight.
I think she's a little young to have a date.
I don't see how we can afford that.
It's fine. I just don't have any appetite.
I thought we'd watch it together. It starts at eight.
I still don't understand what you're getting at.
There are things I can do and things I can't.
It's been longer than that. Like a couple of weeks.
I told you about it. You said to go ahead.
She's just someone I know. She works at the plant.
I thought you fixed it. Listen. It still squeaks.
In one of those boxes probably under the bed.
I still don't understand what you're getting at.
You ought to tell the doctor about your cough.
She's going to be with people we don't know.
I just can't believe you did that.
Three more men on the shift have been laid off.
Let the dog back in before you go.

A Walk in the Woods

Tell me the difference in women and men.
A chromosome. And something else.
Between a romantic and classical heart.
The temperature at which it melts.

Between the secular and the zealous.
The literate person as a rule
is not zealous; the zealous is not
literate. Either can be a fool.

Between important and trivial things.
If you would like to want to live
forever go read Woolf and Welty
and Yeats and Hardy and time will forgive

the time you spent on Sunday puzzles.
Or, if you're sad at dying so soon,
go sit in front of the television
from breakfast till five in the afternoon.

In times that were and times that are.
The streets were not so young and wild
and people sat on porches and every
adult was the parent of every child.

A lawyer knew Latin if not the law.
A doctor would not just cure a disease
but heal the patient. Lawyers wore galluses.
We were in awe of their degrees.

In left and right. They both believe
in greater freedom. They disagree
only on the finer point
of what it means to be free.

In us and others. They look at us
from places we can never stand.
In you and me. Ah, my child,
we've wandered longer than I had planned.

For J. William Fulbright
on the Day of His Death

Walking the square in a tree-thick mountain town
in Arkansas, a visitor is shown
a face and a few words, a monument
in bronze and stone,

a good and visible and local sign
of all the good he left us, something to touch,
but other monuments will last as long
and say as much.

Think of students with minds made darkly rich
by cultures not their own, and who can say—
given the sweet contagion of a thought—
how far away

the tremors of opening minds may resonate?
Beyond our great-grandchildren? Further than that?
Socrates taught young Plato at whose student's feet
we all have sat

through forty increasingly nervous centuries
while those rare minds turned other minds around.
Then think of the hundreds of nations, talking and talking,
the endless sound

of words, words, in every language words,
old terrible words but better than bombs by far.
This brave cacophony, he brought about.
All that we are—

fumbling and noble, enduring, uncertain, and weak—
this body of nations embodies: the foulest and best,
imperfect memory, fear, the one long hope,
and the half-expressed

deep rage of half the world, brought barely together:
one simple resolution, his gift to earth;
some words, when we had little faith in what
words could be worth.

Then think that every time, alone in darkness,
someone finds the courage to take a stand
against the arrogance of power or lifts
one hesitant hand

against the tyranny of mad momentum,
there is a monument. And there. And there.
And there, in a thought that seems at times too simple
for us to bear,

that peace is a progress moving first in the mind,
something left a little more clear
in the heads of the heads of state and common people
because he was here.

What shall we say, now that he's not among us?
We might speak for a moment as if he were.
We might take once his imagined hand and say,
We'll miss you, Sir.

Wide Place in the Road

At last when he had to go back
to be at one of those funerals he had to attend,
he knew how it would be,
hugging his aunts and asking about a friend

he hadn't thought of in years,
everyone saying he surely was a sight
for sore eyes and such,
how kind he was to come. But he found a seat

alone on the back bench.
He watched the dresses, the plodding blue overalls,
the white shirts stiffly clean,
new canvas shoes on all the whispering girls.

The preacher kept on saying,
"Eternal bliss awaits you and I."
Then he saw with discomfort
that only he and the preacher wore a tie.

He thought of slipping it off,
wadding it into his pocket, but then he thought, No.
He had to be what he was,
not what his father was too long ago.

Aunts and uncles and cousins,
he wasn't sure that these were why he came,
or why, since he had come,
it somehow made him nervous to put his name

in the little book at the door,
or if he imagined the looks of reprimand.
He had a long drive home.
If he didn't stop at the grave they would understand.

He knew he had another thirty years
and that's if he was lucky. He might have less
but that didn't bother him much. He had his turn.
One death in the endless turning was little loss.

The pattern stayed, the tapestry went on,
and buried somewhere in the warp and weave
some twist of a thread would say that he was here
if only long enough to stand and wave

and step away. He went gladly to work
and worked his deals as if he didn't care
that he was temporary. He watched the news
and loved his wife and bought a bigger car.

But when he learned that all the universe,
now like a spreading hand, would close to a fist
in a billion years then disappear completely,
he knew that he'd been tricked. He'd never faced

the prospect of a time past all of time
with no one left to wonder about the days
when he was here, to marvel at old bones
the way he did but now no longer does.

Now, driving home, he thinks how silly cars are,
how useless it is, and necessary, now that he's here,
to take the garbage out, and brush his teeth,
and cover up the gray in his thinning hair.

If Ever There Was One

She could tell he loved her. He wanted her there
sitting in the front pew when he preached.
He liked to watch her putting up her hair
and ate whatever she cooked and never broached

the subject of the years before they met.
He was thoughtful always. He let her say
whether or not they did anything in bed
and tried to learn the games she tried to play.

She could tell how deep his feeling ran.
He liked to say her name and bought her stuff
for no good reason. He was a gentle man.
How few there are she knew well enough.

He sometimes reached to flick away a speck
of something on her clothes and didn't drum
his fingers on the table when she spoke.
What would he do if he knew she had a dream

sometimes, slipping out of her nightgown—
if ever God forbid he really knew her—
to slip once out of the house and across town
and find someone to talk dirty to her.

Ballad of a Little Delta Town

They said their vows in the Church of the Pentecost
and she had blushed a little when they kissed.
She'd got her a good man, who everyone knew
would do most anything you asked him to.
He fought the fire when the neighbor's toolshed burned
and wasn't the last to call the time he learned
a distant relative had come to harm,
but he had difficulty being warm.
He sometimes said the words but they sounded flat.
At first she sort of pitied him for that.
She told herself she was lucky to have his love
and a double-wide, that it was blessing enough
just to touch his hand as she fell asleep.
Year by year, though, as the chill ran deep,
she felt her feelings harden and grow brittle.
She took a job to be out of the house a little.

In the only café in the twelve-block delta town
a man lumbered up to the counter and spraddled down.
She brought him coffee and wiped the counter clean.
He talked like someone out of a magazine.
He was as sure of himself as a true believer,
smart as a quarterback, quick as a wide receiver.
Smarter than many, she'd always thought she knew
the way to read the winds, however they blew,
and knew as she knew her name that nothing is free
but took his touch for the truth it seemed to be.

Between a stand of maple and lowing cows
she felt for leaves in her hair and buttoned her blouse.
He took his 18-wheeler out of town.

What's done is done, she said. She let herself down
as carefully as she could to her frightening door,
thinking of what she wasn't anymore.

She put her nightgown on and sat on the bed.
Half the glass of bleach fell over the spread.

Her husband found her lying in a sprawl
as if the bed had caught her in a fall.

When neighbors and kin leaned toward him in his loss
he leaned away. Someone standing across
from where he stood at the coffin might have said
that he looked sad or not at all sad,
that his lower lip tightened and started to curl
much like the lip of a person thinking cruel
thoughts or someone trying not to cry,
and no one heard him say, Good-bye, good-bye.

An Old Man Leaves His Church
for the Last Time

It's all about tithing now.

What happened to the gospel way
of getting saved?

Before, when people got saved
they stopped doing the way they used to do.
They had new ways to live,
not a part of this world.

Today people say they're going
to live like Christians
but still they go to dances,
they go to movies,
still they live the way they used to live.

How do they ever expect to shine their light?

Jesus wants us to witness by words and works
and also how we dress.

The Bible tells us, "Be ye separate people."

And where is the preacher of holiness or hell?
Before, whenever sinners came to church
there was a pulling spirit, they felt something.
Now it's nothing but altar committee
and tithing.

Let me tell you, it's holiness or hell.

I know I get on the nerves
of worldly people.

Let me ask you, though,
if you were standing alone at the edge of town
and saw a rolling cloud coming toward you,
what kind of a person would you be
if you didn't call out in the streets
that a cloud was coming?

Part 3

Admonitions

. . . Not that I'll care,
but I'm moved to now for then.

—John Ciardi

For All Our Great-Grandchildren

when you are grown
with eyes and names I wish I could have known
and more real now than I, but how to begin
speaking to you, our sweet and future kin?

You're each the only one there is of you.
This is not to tell you something new,
but think about the responsibility
of being the only one you will ever be.
Treat your mind and body with the care
you ought to spend on anything that rare.

Forgive yourself. No other forgiving is more
necessary or harder to beg for.

Be nearly too stubborn to change, but never quite.
Be kind, when you can. When you cannot, be right.

Live with the knowledge that living takes its toll
till soon or late we spin out of control,
regardless of obligation, love, or law.

Wherever you are, the moon or Arkansas,
I felt you close today. Don't pay much mind.
The dead will rattle on. The world's designed
to have us rattle. So here, in hope and love,
some things I'd say if I were still alive
and if you asked, which obviously you have not.
And you have things to do. What we've got

is a great-grandfather with too much to say,
and great-grandchildren alive in their own day
and little channel between them. If you can listen
I'll try to make it not sound like a lesson.

A Story

When an act of kindness is not done
as it might have been done it doesn't behoove one
to fuss about it. As she who now would be
your great-great-great-grandmother put it to me
when I complained that my sister, who made it for love,
hadn't gotten the soup hot enough
(putting her arm around her granddaughter),
"Them that never goes to draw the water
won't ever leave the bucket in the well."

She could cipher some but she couldn't spell
past her own name.

                    I guess in the summer
when I turned twelve I left a wrench and a hammer
lying where I'd worked a while on my bike.
I can hear the words that called me back
as if she had said them to me yesterday:
"The job ain't done till you put your tools away."

She taught me *hear* from *heed, poorly* from *sick,*
right from wrong, that couldn't read a lick.
I figured it out, though. If now she could not,
she knew how once but grew so old she forgot.
I wondered about the books she must have read
when she was young to carry in her head,
now that she was old, the things that she knew.
I looked in my dreams to find them. I still do.

Money

Money is flesh and bone. Honestly got,
money is one's own toil, time, and thought
in tangible form. Money unfairly had
is somebody else's labor and should go bad
in any pocket or wallet or bank vault.
Should but doesn't. It isn't money's fault
if it doesn't care whose purse or pocket it fills.
It makes people agree and pays bills,
not knowing whether it was earned or won,
stolen or borrowed. It does what it's always done,
clamshells to plastic cards, a little better
for the creditor than for the debtor.

Buying and Selling

People have dangled like fish on hooks that were baited
by others who took their need to be inflated
and offered it back to them as promise and praise.
This can be done in a numberless number of ways—
by a shape in a bar that saw you come in alone,
a money-hunting voice on a telephone,
the people whose catalog you're amazed to get,
the woman trading you up to a bigger set,
just dollars more a month a few months longer.
Each one of these comprehends the hunger
to be someone deserving closer attention.
We comprehend it ourselves. It is ancient.
We could say, "We know your game," but then
we'd be confused, alone, and hungry again.
Part of what we pay, we pay for the car.
The rest we pay to be told who we are.

Few things are more liberating to learn
than this: that when it's none of their concern
who ask you, "What do you do?" or "How much did you pay?"
it's not a lie, no matter what you say.
If they don't have any right to know,
tell them anything that isn't so.
In a lowered voice, it's like shelter and food
to nosy people and better than being rude.

Self-Control

Much comes out of the body and, by and large,
you'll be more comfortable if you're in charge,
deciding what and when the best you can,
and so will others be. There was a man
who never said a thing he didn't mean.
To him all mindless sounds were obscene,
and empty words especially profane,
signifying a failure in the brain.
He'd never said a word he had to regret.
The fact is, he was less likely to let
a rash or indeliberate word pass
than feel impromptu solid, liquid, or gas
part from his darkness in public. Even sweat.

He was profoundly embarrassed at anything wet
coming unbidden out of the body. Hence,
he saw tears as a form of incontinence.
He nearly forgave the flesh its watery art;
worse were unmeasured words, the brain's fart.

He was a model of calm and eloquence,
a man of obvious breeding and good sense,
well known far beyond the neighborhood.
His children all left home as soon as they could.

Origami

It's wise to know one's self enough to share
a bed without embarrassment. Don't stare
too long at what you are. A woman once
was so concerned with how the psyche runs
she'd start to think a thought and watch the chain
of math and fire go skipping through her brain—
the silent explosions, the bright electric pools,
the spin and wobble of the molecules.
She watched herself watching herself reflect
till thought and thought began to intersect.
Whereupon
she folded into herself and she was gone.

Compassion

Have compassion for everyone you meet
even if they don't want it. What seems conceit,
bad manners, or cynicism is always a sign
of things no ears have heard, no eyes have seen.
You do not know what wars are going on
down there where the spirit meets the bone.

Agreeing

The flower is red, or yellow, as the case may be,
but you and everybody else agree
on which it is, and whose eyes are blue.
What does it mean that people agree with you?
There's no way that you can know you mean
the same color when two of you say, "Green,"
though colors, of course, are not what this is about.
No point in going on and spelling it out.

Caution

The odds can be terribly tempting. All the same,
be careful of the other person's game.
If someone offers you a deck of cards
and bets you anything the Jack of Hearts
will pop out and punch you in the nose,
sing "Moon River" and take off all his clothes,
then run around the room passing his hat,
don't take the bet. He'll do exactly that.

How It's Born in Us to Understand That
There Are Two Sides to Every Question

Think how we predators to every creature,
watching a TV show on the ways of nature,
a rabbit chased through snow by a beast of prey,
always root for the rabbit to get away.

War and Peace

Peace is something most often to be preferred
to confrontation for nations or lovers. The word
can be confusing, though, like a mockingbird.
You can hear it and not know what you've heard.
"Peace, at last!" you sigh. Which is to say
there won't be any violence today?
But there is the peace of death, of indifference,
of fear, of exhaustion, the peace of good sense,
and sometimes the peace of love. You'll want to find out
what peace it is before you spread it about.

Dust

There is a sadness so deep
the sun seems black
and you don't have to try to keep
the tears back

because you couldn't cry
if you wanted to.
Even your thoughts are dry.
All you can do

is stare at the ceiling
and wish the world would mend
and try to recall some better feeling
to no good end.

The Office Party

A monastery's careful austerity,
a mortuary's air of Gethsemane,
can only hint at the feel of the first few hours
back at work while memory churns and sours
after an office party that got too loose.
No glance was ever quicker or more abstruse
than those across the phones and keyboards
where people exchange their obligatory reports
with mumbling politeness and, meeting in doorways,
give way too far, step back with too much grace.
Some count their paper clips to break the spells
of those who whispered of meals and motels.

Beware of such a party and take care
that when a hand slides into underwear
the reasons it found its way last longer than all
the music and drinks and lapse of protocol.

God

Call evil all that debases the human spirit
for physical pleasure, for money, for power, for sport,
for simple convenience. Call a spirit debased
when someone has hurt a person or other beast
or the earth, its water, its air, the breathing plants,
without necessity and reverence.

Call what enriches the human spirit, good.

This will serve unless you say that God
has first to be written in as a Final Cause.
Fine, then. Say that God fashioned us all
after His image, that we are obliged by the Fall
to walk barefoot on the gravelly fields of faith
because we spoiled the spirit that was His breath.

But don't thank God for food, for bringing you through
the operation nearly as good as new,
for the tired swimmer safe, the soldier at ease.
You can't give God the credit for any of these
unless you hold Him accountable for the rest—
the mouth indifferent on the shrunken breast,
the soldier bagged, the swimmer in free fall,
the patient dead on the table. God did it all
or does nothing. To save a child from disease,
to bless a boat of ragbone refugees,
means choosing to turn from others, one by one.
God decides for all of us, or none.

Think, read, and pray, but there are only three
barely possible ways for God to be:

He may shape the fortunes of a few,
leaving the rest to falter or stumble through,
or He may plan it all, the watered shares,
the brakes in time, the toy at the top of the stairs.
But these are the same: if some are in His hands
then all are there, and neither law nor chance
is what we thought. Love, rage, neglect, or whim,
everything that happens falls to Him,
who keeps the carnal existence and the soul
of every person under His control,
stripping the flesh of one and stroking another.
No matter how much we believe the author
should love what is written down, who are we
to question how the universe should be?

Or say that He leaves us to chance and the love we find,
and takes no hand and possibly pays no mind.

Or say that He doesn't exist. Then what?

Think as we will of His nature or that He is not,
on what we believe about Him, in the end,
much more than our theologies depend.
Also most of politics, and much
of schoolroom and courtship and courtroom. The ways we touch.

Memory

You can't keep all of the past in a backpack or purse
all of the time. It's heavy, and what's worse,
it wouldn't leave room for much else,
what with drive-in movies, wooden motels,
a record player with needles, a touring car.
But what we were is much of what you are,
and what you are . . . believe me when I say
that what you are is going to wear away
little by little until, to your awful surprise,
you aren't all there; you barely recognize
what's left. Go now and rummage back to find
some odds and ends that may have been consigned
to dusty boxes somewhere in the mind.
Put them together and make of them a book
with ragged, bone-white leaves and a leather look.
Use whatever is there—how it was to spend
a long while in silence with a friend,
to watch the trembling death of a dog, to look
with wonder on the ordinary, to like
the feel in the flesh of time passing, to be
your crowded selves with nothing more from me.
I can't say what you'll find for stuff and glue.
I don't know all that you're made of. I hope you do.

Part 4

The
Inaugural
Poem

Read by the poet
at the inauguration of
William Jefferson Clinton,
January 20, 1997

Of History and Hope

We have memorized America,
how it was born and who we have been and where.
In ceremonies and silence we say the words,
telling the stories, singing the old songs.
We like the places they take us. Mostly we do.
The great and all the anonymous dead are there.
We know the sound of all the sounds we brought.
The rich taste of it is on our tongues.
But where are we going to be, and why, and who?
The disenfranchised dead want to know.
We mean to be the people we meant to be,
to keep on going where we meant to go.

But how do we fashion the future? Who can say how
except in the minds of those who will call it Now?
The children. The children. And how does our garden grow?
With waving hands—oh, rarely in a row—
and flowering faces. And brambles, that we can no longer allow.

Who were many people coming together
cannot become one people falling apart.
Who dreamed for every child an even chance
cannot let luck alone turn doorknobs or not.
Whose law was never so much of the hand as the head
cannot let chaos make its way to the heart.
Who have seen learning struggle from teacher to child
cannot let ignorance spread itself like rot.
We know what we have done and what we have said,
and how we have grown, degree by slow degree,
believing ourselves toward all we have tried to become—
just and compassionate, equal, able, and free.

All this in the hands of children, eyes already set
on a land we never can visit—it isn't there yet—
but looking through their eyes, we can see
what our long gift to them may come to be.
If we can truly remember, they will not forget.

Miller Williams, University Professor of English and Foreign Languages at the University of Arkansas as well as director of the University of Arkansas Press, is the author, co-author, or translator of twenty-eight books, including twelve poetry collections. He has received a number of literary awards, among them the Poets' Prize, the Prix de Rome for Literature of the American Academy of Arts and Letters, the Academy Award for Literature of the American Academy of Arts and Letters, the Amy Lowell Award in Poetry, the Henry Bellaman Poetry Prize, the New York Arts Fund Award for Distinguished Contribution to American Letters, and the John William Corrington Award for Literary Excellence. A native of Arkansas, he was born in Hoxie, spent his formative years in Russellville and Fort Smith, and graduated from Arkansas State University and the University of Arkansas. He has also taught at McNeese State College, Louisiana State University, Loyola University in New Orleans, and—as Fulbright Professor of American Studies—at the University of Mexico. At the request of President Clinton, he served as the 1997 Inaugural Poet, delivering on January 20 a poem written for the occasion.

Dear John, Dear Coltrane
Michael S. Harper (1985)

Poems from the Sangamon
John Knoepfle (1985)

In It
Stephen Berg (1986)

The Ghosts of Who We Were
Phyllis Thompson (1986)

Moon in a Mason Jar
Robert Wrigley (1986)

Lower-Class Heresy
T. R. Hummer (1987)

Poems: New and Selected
Frederick Morgan (1987)

Furnace Harbor: A Rhapsody of
the North Country
Philip D. Church (1988)

Bad Girl, with Hawk
Nance Van Winckel (1988)

Blue Tango
Michael Van Walleghen (1989)

Eden
Dennis Schmitz (1989)

Waiting for Poppa at the
Smithtown Diner
Peter Serchuk (1990)

Great Blue
Brendan Galvin (1990)

What My Father Believed
Robert Wrigley (1991)

Something Grazes Our Hair
S. J. Marks (1991)

Walking the Blind Dog
G. E. Murray (1992)

The Sawdust War
Jim Barnes (1992)

The God of Indeterminacy
Sandra McPherson (1993)

Off-Season at the Edge of the
World
Debora Greger (1994)

Counting the Black Angels
Len Roberts (1994)

Oblivion
Stephen Berg (1995)

To Us, All Flowers Are Roses
Lorna Goodison (1995)

Honorable Amendments
Michael S. Harper (1995)

Points of Departure
Miller Williams (1995)

Dance Script with Electric
Ballerina
Alice Fulton (reissue, 1996)

To the Bone: New and Selected
Poems
Sydney Lea (1996)

Floating on Solitude
Dave Smith (3-volume reissue,
1996)

Bruised Paradise
Kevin Stein (1996)

Walt Whitman Bathing
David Wagoner (1996)

Rough Cut
Thomas Swiss (1997)

Paris
Jim Barnes (1997)

The Ways We Touch
Miller Williams (1997)

National Poetry Series

Eroding Witness
  Nathaniel Mackey (1985)
  Selected by Michael S. Harper

Palladium
  Alice Fulton (1986)
  Selected by Mark Strand

Other Poetry Volumes